THE ULTIMATE Hannukah ACTIVITY BOOK

Hannukah History, Activities, Puzzles and MORE!

The Ultimate Hanukkah Activity Book
By E.V. Pepper
Copyright 2017 Pizza Monster Press

ISBN-13: 978-1979568579
ISBN-10: 197956857X

No part of this book, including images in part or whole, may be reproduced or distributed in any form or by any means, without prior written permission of the author.

HISTORY OF HANNUKAH

Every year in November/December Jewish people world wide spend eight nights lighting candles, celebrating, singing, eating donuts and playing with dreidels.

In Hebrew, the word "Hanukkah" means "dedication." It reminds us that this holiday celebrates the rededication of the Holy Temple in Jerusalem following the Maccabee victory over the Seleucid army in 165 BCE (Before the Christian Era).

Hanukkah lasts for eight nights, during which we light a candle every night. We light these candles to remember the miracle that occurred in 165 BCE. In that year the Seleucid, a group of Syrian-Greeks, ruled over Jerusalem. They made it very difficult to practice Judaism and even made many Jewish traditions illegal!

The Seleucid put up a statue of Zeus in the holy Jewish temple and sacrificed pigs there! The Maccabees a strong tribe of Jewish rebels led by Judah Maccabee, were horrified by the disrespect. They said "Enough is Enough!" The Maccabees fought a giant army of Syrian-Greeks for control of Jerusalem but during the battle the holy temple was destroyed. The Maccabees reclaimed what was left of the temple but they only had one tiny jar of lamp oil left. They lit a lamp to rededicate the new temple and this tiny jar lasted for 8 days!

* Imagine if your cell phone was at 10% and lasted for 8 whole days! Now you know what hannukah feels like!

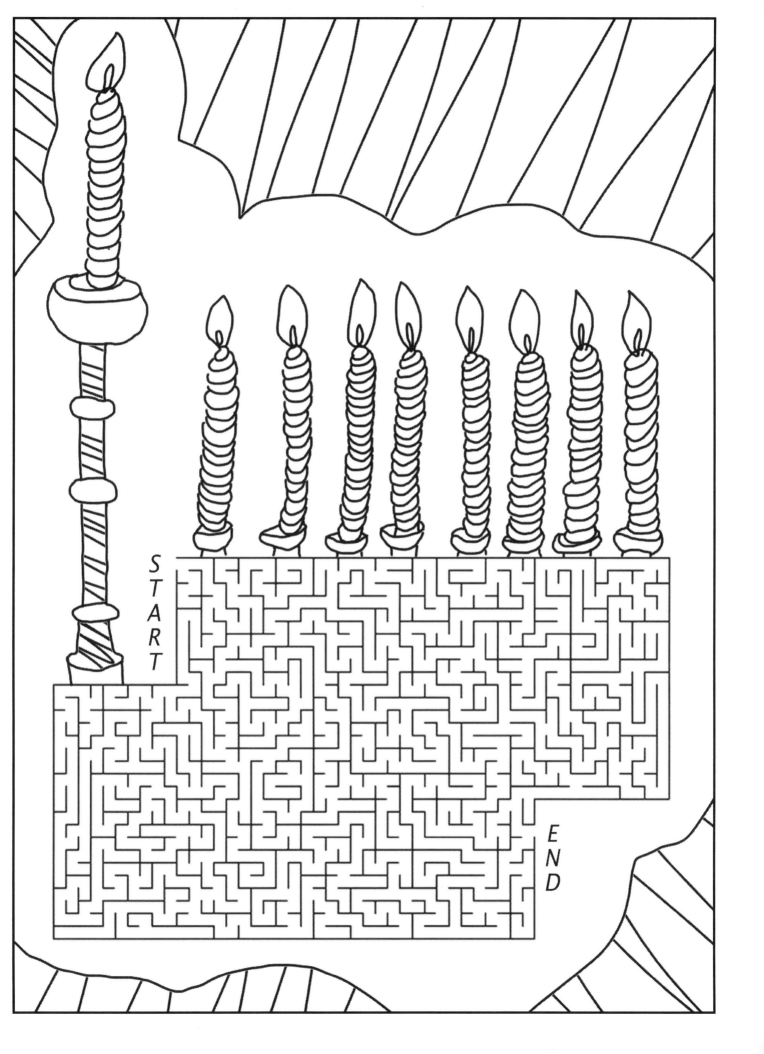

HOW DO WE LIGHT THE CANDLES?

A chanukia is the menorah we use only on Hanukkah. It has nine arms: eight for each night the miracle oil burned, and one for the shamash, which is the "helper" candle. The shamash is typically higher than the other candles, and is the one you light first. Then, each night at sundown you use the shamash to light the other candles.

You restart with fresh candles every night: Night one, you place a candle on the far right of the chanukia and light it with the shamash. Night two, you place a candle in the far right of the Chanukia and add a candle to its left. Then light the new candle first with the shamash. Night three, you add a third candle on the left and light that one first, then the second, then the third. Repeat the process until you light eight candles on the eighth night!

YOU'LL NEED TO LIGHT 44 CANDLES DURING HANUKKAH

Before World War II, on the last night of Hanukkah in Germany all the leftover wicks and oil in a neighborhood were gathered and lit in a giant bonfires. People sang songs and danced around the fire, often until the small hours of the night.

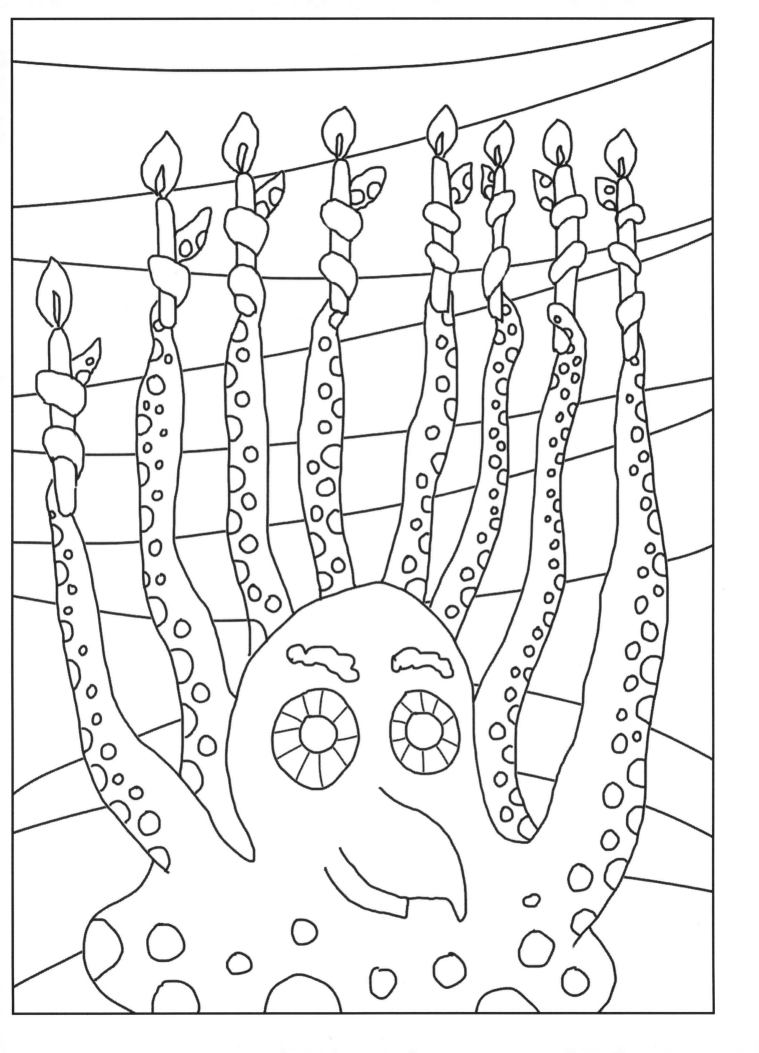

HOW DO WE SPELL CHANUKKA?!?!?

In hebrew, Hanukkah means "dedication" after the Maccabee reclaimed the holy temple in Jerusalem. Today Hanukkah is often referred to as the "Festival of Lights" because of all the candles we light. However you may have see the word Hanukkah spelled many different ways. Channuka, Hanukka, Hanukkah, Hannuka. What gives?

Well, the original word is written in Hebrew which has a different alphabet then english. So "hanukkah" is transliterated from Hebrew using the closest letters in the english language. There is no exact Enlish letter equivalent for the sounds Hebrew letters make. Technically we could even spell it Khanoooccah and we wouldn't actually be wrong.

THIS HOLIDAY IS HUGE!

Actually Hanukkah isn't the biggest Jewish holiday! There is no mention of Hanukkah in the Torah. Judaism places much more importance on Passover and Rosh Hashanah (the Jewish New Year). However, Hanukkah often falls in December and thats when the majority of people are celebrating Christmas. Jews in the United States began to place more and more importance on Hanukka in the 20th century and today most Jews around the world celebrate Hanukkah as a major holiday.

THE REAL HANUKKAH MIRACLE — SPELLING HANUKKAH CORRECTLY!

HANEROT HALALU
(Traditional Hanukkah song)

Hanerot halalu, anu madlikin
Al hanisim ve'al hanifla'ot
Ve'al hateshu'ot, ve'al hamilchamot
She'asita la'avoteinu
Bayamim haheim bazman hazeh
Al yedei kohanecha hak'doshim.

V'chol sh'monat yemei Chanukah (x2)
Hanerot halalu, hanerot halalu kodesh heim.
Ve'ein lanu reshut lehishtameish bahem
Ela lir'otam bilvad
Kedei lohodot ulehalleil leshimcha hagadol
Al nissehcha ve'al yeshuatehcha
Ve'al nifle'otehcha.

(ENGLISH VERSION)
THESE CANDLES

These Chanukah lights we kindle
In honor of the miracles, the wonders
And salvation wrought and wars
You fought, for our fathers,
In days of yore and in present time (x2)
By the hands of Your holy priests.

And throughout Chanukah's eight days
These lights, these lights shall be sacred:
No right to make use of them have we
Only to look at them and see,
That Your great Name we may thank and praise
For the miracles and salvation You brought
And for Your wondrous deeds.

WHAT IS A MENORAH?

A Menorah is the traditional jewish eight armed candle holder, but on Hanukkah we usually use a Chanukia! This is a menorah with nine arms! The traditional eight arms represent each night the miracle oil burned bright in the temple. The extra ninth arm is called the Shamash and is used to light the other eight candles during Hanukkah.

Traditionally the menorah is placed outside the front door or, as is the custom today, displayed in the window of every Jewish home. (Watch out for those flammable curtains!)

FACT
Menorahs Cause 10% More Fires in Jerusalem during Hanukka!

WHO IS THE SHAMASH?

In hebrew the Shamash mean "servant" or "helper". It is used to help light the other candles. The Shamash is typically higher and kept apart from the other candles. During each night of hanukka we light the shamash first and use it to light each other candle. Do not light your Hanukkah candles with other Hanukkah candles!

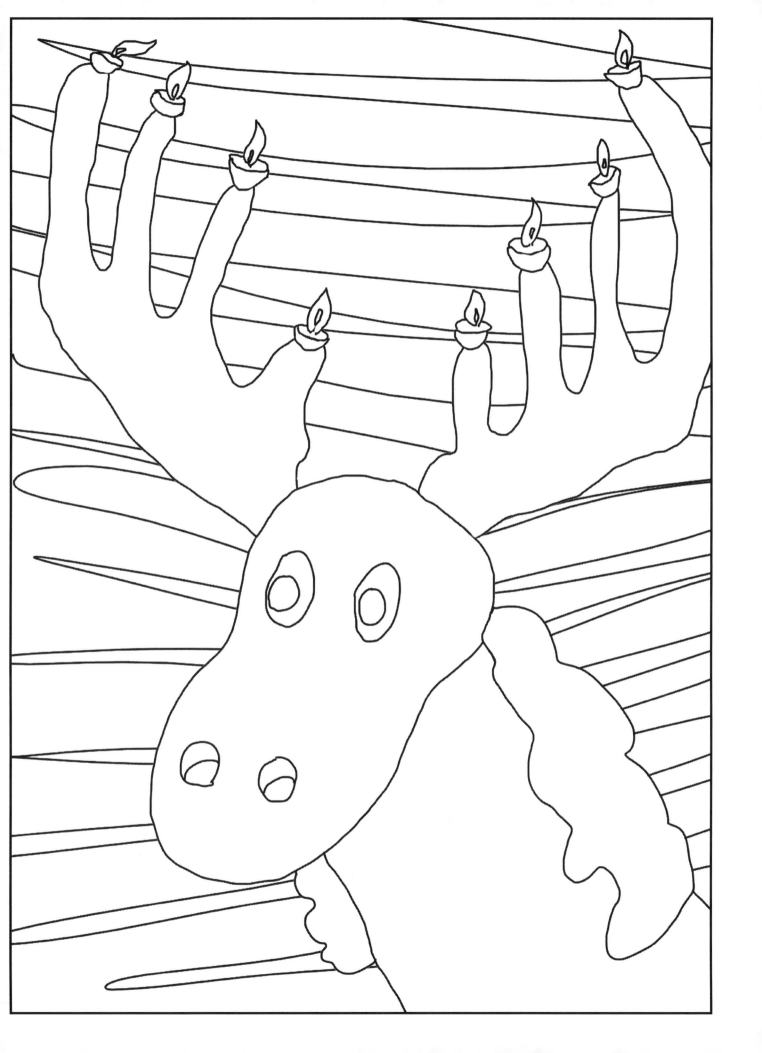

HANUKKAH MUSIC AND SONGS

Music plays a huge role in most Jewish holidays. Some have more traditional songs associated with them than others. Traditional songs for Hanukkah are "I have a little dreidel" (the hebrew version is "Sevivon Sof Sof Sof") and HaNerot Hallalu. Since Christmas songs are so abundant, there has been a slew of invented Hanukkah songs like "Hanukkah, Oh Hanukkah" and the Adam Sandler "The Chanukah Song".

CANDLE FACT!

Some people take candle lighting to the next level! Besides buying candles in different color there are scented candles available specifically for menorahs. These scented candles come in vanilla, raspberry, or even sufganiyot flavor!

GIVE ME THE FOOOOOOD!

To celebrate the Hanukkah holiday, we traditionally fry foods in oil to acknowledge the miracle of the oil that lasted eight nights!

Some popular Hunukkah dishes are:
LATKES: potato pancakes served with apple sauce.
SUFGANIYOT: Jelly donuts.
KUGEL: A pudding casserole made with egg noodles.
GELT: Chocolate Coins.

Food Scramble!

- GLABE
- MTZAO
- HACHALL
- KELTA
- LEUKG
- ELEITFG
- KISNH
- TIASAPRM
- FEALAFL
- GUEHRLAC
- LIBIN
- HUMUMS
- BAAKB

D _ _ _ _ _ _ _ _ _

Unscramble each of the clue words.
Take the letters that appear in ◯ boxes and unscramble them for the final message.

```
F M E E J R W Q V O C S N K N
C I R V E E I G H T L U D J T
Q S I Y S E L D N A C V S E B
A J A G R H A L H T G G T L J
F R I E D L A E Y O E A U Q D
P F O T F T B M T P L N N T M
T S Q N K R I D M O T I O Q J
T A U E E B A C C A M Y D P Y
G G E W O M F O M P S A I A H
G N C E E S H J F A Y H P Y Y
A L Q N J C K T U F S F R C W
M G R R Q C E G F R X N E P L
C D G K T V D Z O P T G E O Q
R Y L O M Y G W B L E S P I E
Y I A K N B Q Q V G V Z L T L
```

AMEN	CANDLES	CHOCOLATE
DONUTS	EIGHT	FRIED
GELT	GIFT	HEBREW
HOLIDAY	JELLY	LATKE
MACCABEE	MENORA	POTATO
PRAYER	SHAMMASH	SUVGANIYAH
WORSHIP		

DREIDEL

During Hanukkah there is one major entertainment. Thats Dreidel! The Dreidel or Sevivon is a small four sided spinning top with hebrew characters printed on the side. It is said that before th Maccabees revolted, Jews were not legally allowed to read hebrew! So to study the Tora they would sneak Hebrew into simple games such as the Dreidel. Each of the four sides of a dreidel has a Hebrew character: Nun, Gimel, Hay or Shin. The four letters stand for the phrase "Nes Gadol Hayah Sham"—meaning "A great miracle happened there"—which refers to the miraculous, long-lasting oil in Jerusalem.

DREIDEL SONG

"I have a little dreidel,

"I made it out of clay,

"And when it's dry and ready,

"A dreidel game I'll play:'

(This song goes way back and is sung to celebrate Hanukkah. Today Dreidels are made of plastic, but we still sing and remember the first clay dreidels that the Maccabee children played with long ago.)

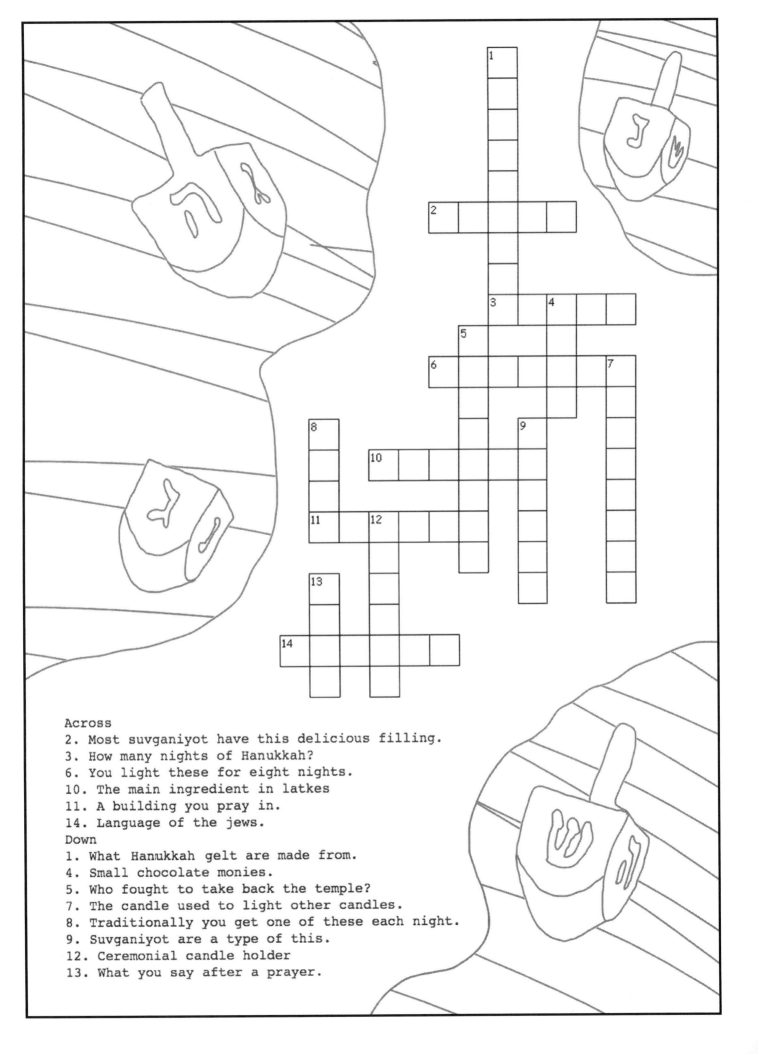

Across
2. Most suvganiyot have this delicious filling.
3. How many nights of Hanukkah?
6. You light these for eight nights.
10. The main ingredient in latkes
11. A building you pray in.
14. Language of the jews.

Down
1. What Hanukkah gelt are made from.
4. Small chocolate monies.
5. Who fought to take back the temple?
7. The candle used to light other candles.
8. Traditionally you get one of these each night.
9. Suvganiyot are a type of this.
12. Ceremonial candle holder
13. What you say after a prayer.

WHEN IS HANUKKAH?

The original date for Hanukkah is based on the Hebrew calendar, and like the spelling there is no direct correlation between our Gregorian calendar. Hanukkah always falls on the 25th day of the Hebrew month Kislev, and that can fall anywhere between late November to late December!

JUST GIVE ME THE GIFTS!

In the past, Jews traditionally celebrated Hanukkah by giving their kids "gelt" (the yiddish word for money). However, since wrapped gifts play such a big role in Christmas and Secular holiday time, many Jews have switched to this custom and give a Hanukkah. Today Hanukkah Gelt are chocolate coins covered in gold or silver wrappers. They still given during Hanukkah and used for playing the fast paced game of Dreidel.

The chocolate coins known as Gelt appeared around 1920.

Historically, Hanukkah was the time when children were encouraged and rewarded for their hard work studying the Torah. It became a custom to give children Hanukkah money (Gelt) and small presents during the holiday.

SOME YIDDISH WORDS

Yiddish is an ancient language used by Ashkenazi Jews dating back to the 9th century. It is a mix of German, Hebrew, and Aramaic.

Kissel – A little bit. "You want more Latkes" "Just a bissel."
Bubbe – Grandmother "My Bubbe makes the best Latkes!"
Chutzpah – Someone who has extreme nerve and a little arrogant. "He thinks he's the best at Dreidel, what Chutzpah!"
Daven – To Pray
Klutz – A clumsy person. "That Klutz spilled all the Manishevitz!"
Kvell – experience pride in someone else.
"You won the Dreidel game! Im kvelling!"
Kvetch – To complain or whine.
"His biggest Kvetch is that the Suvganiyot are too sugary."
Mensch – An honorable person.
"If you were a mensch, you'd let me have the last latke!"
Meschuggene – Crazy or insane.
"He spells Hanukka with a CH, what a Meschuggene!"
Nosh – a small bite to eat.
"Just a small slice of kuggle. I only need a nosh."
Oy vey! – an expression of woe.
"Oy Vey! We ran out of apple sauce for the latkes!"
Putz – A jerk. "My friend thought the menorah was filled with birthday candle and blew them out! What a Putz!"
Tchotchke – a small toy or collectible.
"Bubbe always gives the best Tchotchkes for hannuka presents!"
Tuches – Butt or behind. "Smooth as a babies Tuches!"
Schlep – To travel with great difficulty, often carrying something.
"I had to schlep 300 suvganyot all the way from Bubbes house!"
Schmooze – To make small talk or chat.
"At that hannuka party I Schmoozed with some real putz's!"
Shmatte – A old ragged piece of clothing.
"Its Hanukka! Take off that scmatte and put on something nice!"
Zayde – Grandfather

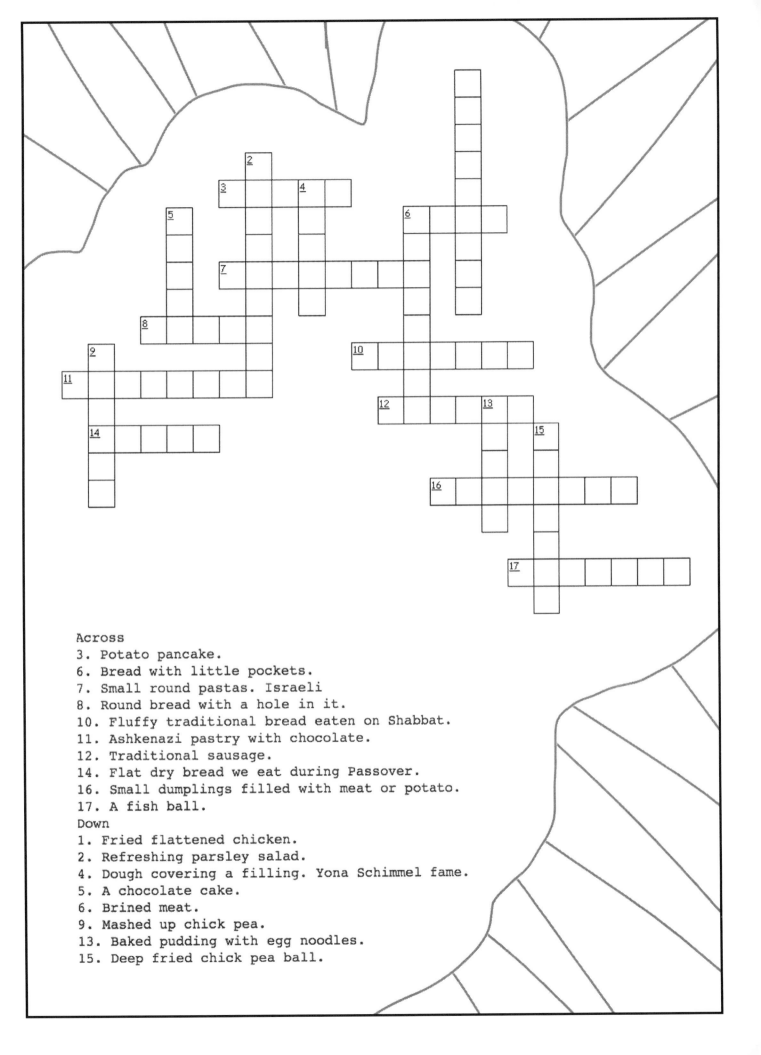

Across
3. Potato pancake.
6. Bread with little pockets.
7. Small round pastas. Israeli
8. Round bread with a hole in it.
10. Fluffy traditional bread eaten on Shabbat.
11. Ashkenazi pastry with chocolate.
12. Traditional sausage.
14. Flat dry bread we eat during Passover.
16. Small dumplings filled with meat or potato.
17. A fish ball.

Down
1. Fried flattened chicken.
2. Refreshing parsley salad.
4. Dough covering a filling. Yona Schimmel fame.
5. A chocolate cake.
6. Brined meat.
9. Mashed up chick pea.
13. Baked pudding with egg noodles.
15. Deep fried chick pea ball.

GRANDMA JOKE!

Last year, just before Hanukkah, Ethel, a grandmother was giving directions to her grown up grandson who was coming to visit with his wife. 'You come to the front door of the apartment building. I am in apartment 2B.'

Ethel continued, 'There is a big panel at the door. With your elbow push button 2B. I will buzz you in. Come inside, the elevator is on the right. Get in, and with your elbow hit 2. When you get out I am on the left. With your elbow, hit my doorbell.'

'Grandma, that sounds easy,'
replied Jonathan, the grandson,
'but why am I hitting all these buttons with my elbow.'

To which she answered,
'You're coming to visit empty handed?'

NOERAM	☐☐☐☐☐☐
PYRREA	☐☐☐☐☐☐
KEATL	☐☐☐☐◯
MEAN	☐☐☐◯
DUTON	☐☐☐☐☐
BEMECCAA	☐☐☐☐◯☐☐☐
LEEDRDI	☐☐☐☐☐☐☐
DANLEC	☐◯☐☐☐☐
NYVGASUTIO	☐◯☐☐☐☐☐☐☐
TEGHI	☐☐☐◯☐
HERWBE	◯☐☐☐☐☐

☐☐☐☐☐K☐☐

Unscramble each of the clue words.

Take the letters that appear in ◯ boxes and unscramble them for the final message.

```
U W I P Y B Y N H L P O Z T Z B H W U S
A W H Y D L G G A Z A R Z B Z S U J V L
B L H I B D J U L U S Y J T T I M D E K
T F A L A F E L L R T X R E A K M G U G
Y A Q V D L C S A X R A Y T F M U M C X
S R B I E L T D H Z A E O X H K S V E L
K U T B E Q K J C R M K H E Z F W H N S
H V O B O M T U M P I T N W Z Z P F A
Y D V C H U W H S S Q A C D I S I N E O
H I Q V S S L R C F H L Z H N T D F L O
L C N Q Y U V E V G N A T G A G S D A Q
X B A V D A O L H S R I I K N Y L D F N
C L W C C O K C F U E W B N B Y H Y V S
R U L R R K J H G T B Q Q C L B J F R D
S C H N I T Z E L G T L O H R A C R K C
T J U S S V L I Q W H W I L W B G L Q R
Y G H S A A F K N I S H I N I K F U R O
X K T T C E M T L C I T G Q I A E C V L
A P S H G S W I X H C A L P E R K H V I
I X M B F L E G A B Z Y V T L F B C O W
```

BABKA	BAGEL	BLINI
CHALLAH	COUSCOUS	FALAFEL
GEFILTE	HUMMUS	KISHKA
KNISH	KREPLACH	KUGEL
LATKE	MATZO	PASTRAMI
PITA	RUGELACH	SCHNITZEL
TABBOULEH	TZIMMES	

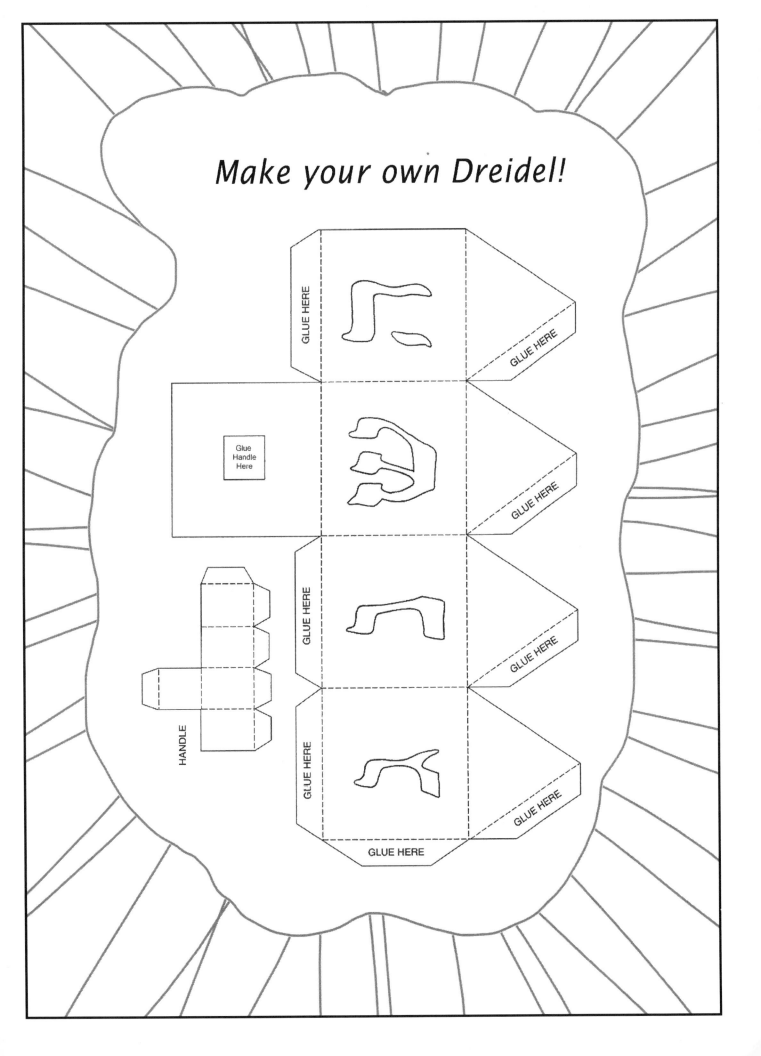

Hebrew Sayings

Happy Birthday
יום הולדת שמח *(Yom hooledet sameiakh)*

I love you
אני אוהב אותך *(Ani ohev otakh)*

Hello
שלום *(Shalom)*

Cool!
סבבה! *(Sababa!)*

Welcome
ברוך הבא *(Baruch Haba)*

My name is...
שמי _____ *(Shmi _____)*...

Good Morning
בוקר טוב *(Boker Tov)*

Good Night
ליל טוב *(Laila Tov)*

Thank you
תודה רבה *(Todah Rabah)*

Enough!
די! *(Dai!)*

Made in the USA
Middletown, DE
25 November 2017